Contents

Five easy loop walks in West Cork's distance from Skibbereen 16 miles,

Dedicated to:
my patient wife, children, friends and dog,
who have made life's roads a pleasure
and lightened my steps on the way.

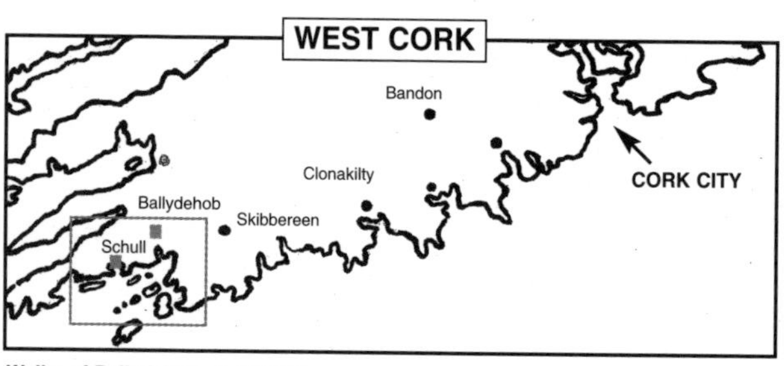

Walks of Ballydehob and Schull

There is no guarantee that a walk outlined in this book is a right-of-way. The author and supporters of this book do not accept any responsibility for trespass nor for accident or loss to or by the public in walking these routes.

A note on walking

The Irish are big on walking. If there is one thing we have plenty of, it is back roads and fresh air.

There are the power walkers, the Walking Women of Ireland, plugging along country roads with hips and shoulders swinging, out for the exercise after an already much-exercised day. The glow of their cheeks and the litheness of their stride attests the beneficial effects of 'exercise walking'.

Irish men, on the other hand, seem oblivious to walking's cosmetic effect, an unfortunate oversight on their part. Males are not seen striding along country lanes. When we do see a male abroad, he is generally being pulled along at a heart-stopping pace by two fist-fulls of dog leads, his greyhounds taking him for a run, rather than the other way around. Other encounters will involve men in caps, with fags in mouth and pockets full of fivers, out following the road bowling, after which they will walk miles.

There are the hill walkers and long-distance route marchers, doughty folk in serious boots, with ashplants, maps and small rucksacks. To them, we owe the opening up of green roads and byways, and the mapping of mountain trails not trodden since the ancient Celts made their way across country via uplands, the plains being covered with a dense growth of trees.

I, myself, do not power walk, greyhound follow, or road bowl wager. I walk for the curiosity and the uplift, the wonderments of the wayside and the 'high' of the free-flowing endorphins released after twenty minutes on the hoof. I am not so much a slow walker as one who is waylaid by the roadside attractions. Curiosity, atmosphere or amazement delays me, and while the company forges ahead, I am left behind, in thrall.

The walks outlined in this book are for walkers such as I. They take, generally, just a couple of hours but can easily be stretched to fill half a day. They are perfect for a weekend afternoon or a holiday meander.

They will, hopefully, stimulate my perambulating neighbours towards new horizons and inform visitors of the lovely land that awaits just off the tourist trail. I cannot imagine these local by-ways ever becoming crowded. We may in time meet a party of ardent Japanese, led by a person with a flag, or stout Austrians in lederhosen and braces singing "Falderee-Falderah". They will be sure of a welcome. We Irish delight in showing off our land.

To the farmers and landowners

In West Cork, the Irish tradition of welcome to passing strangers is still strong. But for the goodwill of farmers and landowners our chance to enjoy the landscape and wild life of the unique Ballydehob-Schull area would be hugely curtailed. While most of the walks outlined in this book are on lanes and back roads, I have also mapped some old tracks, well worn and in use. Where possible, I have spoken personally to the landowners whose ground is crossed. As elsewhere in West Cork, they have not only been co-operative, but wish well to the walker. But, they quite reasonably point out, walkers crossing their property must accept that they do so at their own risk.

I would like, on behalf of all who have ever walked the route over the hill at Colla, to thank the owners of the track that joins the costal public road to the inland public road. This route, with its magnificent views, gives health and pleasure to many. Also, the owners of the old paths and routes at Letter and Rathcool, and those who allow us into their fields to view the ancient monuments.

The area

Beyond Skibbereen, on the R592 going west, the land changes dramatically. The green sward of agribiz stops suddenly at the Roaringwater River, a few miles short of Ballydehob. Beyond it, and from here on, bedrock breaks the fields and there is more gorse than grazing. Now, instead of fence-to-fence nitrate grass bedspreads, the fields are small patchworks, rock-rent and bockety, joined by seams of hedge.

Here, the land is 'free', even if owned, undomesticated, even if farmed. It's a skipping land, up and down and lively as a fiddle air, jigging and reeling as it goes. Much is not worth 'developing', for you can't grow grass on rocks or spuds in bogs It offers little sustenance, and that little is hard won. Of food for the spirit, there is a feast, and if we could live on scenery we'd be satiated. Like the sea or sky, the land here is nature's domain and humans have only scratched the edges. Beyond the roadside fields, the bog stretches away like a brown mantle to the hills or sea. In winter, it is drab as sack-cloth, in summer, it is softened with heather and bright with gorse.

I've walked this countryside many times, especially recently, in preparation for this book. On my routes, the views are always of uplands or islands. On the outward leg, low, brown hills fill the horizon. Beyond them, the mountains of Caha and Kerry rise. On the return, the vast Atlantic is below us, with the small and big islands of Roaringwater Bay.

Little is changed in this part of Ireland. There are farmhouses, holiday homes, and bungalow bliss but, off the bohreens, few feet have walked the rough land. No longer is 90% of what we see changed by Man; now, it is 90% unchanged, altered only by time and nature. Three thousand year ago, paths crossed these local bogs to reach the copper (some say, the gold) workings on Mount Gabriel. They are long since subsumed beneath the brown blanket but, without doubt, the back roads often follow these routes.

Ballydehob and Schull are character-full and pretty settlements. Ballydehob, the smaller, has its strong West Cork 'feel', its imposing twelve arched bridge - last and finest remnant of the West Cork Tramway - its pubs and eating places. Schull has its pier - which serves the islands - its holiday cottages, restaurants, book shops and boutiques. Both are host to passing holiday makers and blow-ins. Ballydehob has, for some years, been home to a small colony of native and expatriate artists, poets and literati, while Schull is a holiday venue for Dublin glitterati, yachtsmen who launch and ladies who lunch.

For all this, the native charm of these West Cork towns is undimmed, the Irish thick on the ground, the arrívistes aping them rather than the other way around. Little change is evident in the surrounding countryside, in the sea, the islands, the hills and the bogs beneath them. We have made small marks on the surface but have little effected the spirit of the place.

Acknowledgements

I am indebted to the following for the kind assistance they gave me in researching this book:

- Mary Mackey and Dr Brian Mackey, Fuschia Books, Schull, enthusiasts and authorities, for their patience and information.

- Members of The Mizen Archaeological and Historical Society, for answering questions put by Mary Mackey on my behalf.

- Ciaran & Deborah O'Carroll, Derryconnel House, Schull, for telling me about the Letter green road.

- Peter Fosse, Peatland Conservation Council, for insights on sedges.

Sources

- The Mizen Journal (various issues) published by The Mizen Archaeological and Historical Society
- A Visitors guide to Schull, Ballydehob, Goleen and The Mizen compiled and published by Schull Development Association.
- Archaeological Inventory of West Cork Vol 1 Government Publications Office, Dublin 1992
- Antiquities of West Cork by Jack Roberts
- The Wild Plants of Sherkin, Cape Clear and adjacent islands of West Cork by John Akeroyd, published by Sherkin Island Marine Station 1996
- Kerry, A Natural History by Terry Carruthers, Collins Press, Cork 1998
- Pond Life by Trevor Beebee, Whittet Books 1992
- Atlas of the Irish Rural Landscape Cork University Press 1997
- The IPPC Guide to Irish Peatlands, Peatland Conservation Council 1988

Roaringwater River Walk

The Roaringwater River - old stone quays where it enters the sea - a McCarthy castle, now home of a movie star - scenic graveyard - ruins of churches.

Locality: OS Sheet 88, starting at 037350, Meen Bridge, on Ballydehob to Skibbereen road about 3 miles east of Ballydehob.

Description and Distance: A loop walk, from sea to uplands. About $4\frac{1}{2}$ miles, with an optional extra of $1\frac{1}{2}$ miles.

Walking Time: $2\frac{1}{2}$ to $3\frac{1}{2}$ hours.

Walking conditions: Little used back roads. A steep stretch for 200 yards, otherwise easy going.

Features: The small creek where the Roaringwater River flows into Roaringwater Bay is almost chocolate-box beautiful, shaded with trees and often mirror flat, with swans. Enclosed, leafy lanes, at first, then open country, with hills in the near distance and fine vistas over Ballydehob Bay. The option takes us to views of a castle in a magnificent location, and a lovely graveyard overlooking the sea.

Flora and fauna: A wonderful diversity of natural history, with coastal, riverine, bogland and moorland species. Rare Lusitanian plants, interesting birds. With luck, an otter.

Equipment: Ordinary walking shoes.

Itinerary:

(1) We turn in off the N71 Skibbereen to Ballydehob road at Aghadown RC church, crossing the ivied bridge on the old road to reach the car park opposite the imposing church. A new bridge, with less character but more strength, carries the N71 over the river just above it. We walk downriver from here.

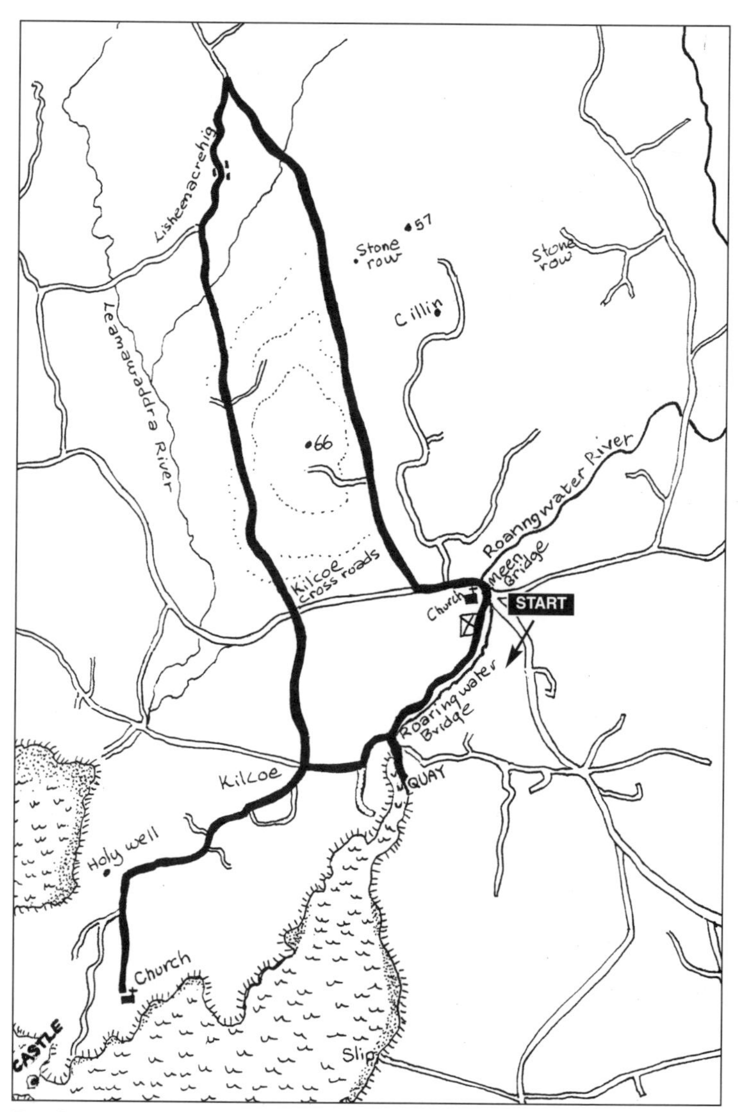

Roaringwater River Walk

The small Roaringwater River, for which the huge bay is named, rises six miles north, on the slopes of Mount Kid. Going west, the next river that feeds the bay is the Leamawaddra, The Dog's Jump River. Dog's Jump Bay would hardly have had the same resonance. The old name was Loch Treasna, Transverse Lake, fine in the Irish, turgid in English.

Opposite, is Kilcoe National School, built 1897. The building is modernised but its surroundings are much like Goldsmith's rural school in 'The Deserted Village' two hundred years ago - "......Beside yon straggling fence that skirts the way. With blossom'd furze unprofitably gay..." Furze indeed blooms gaily on the straggling hedge below it.

It is an idyllic spot for a school. Above is the old bridge, opposite is the river covered in white water crowsfoot in May and June. A large Irish yew, probably as old as the school, shoots shyward through the asphalt in the yard. Yews are slow growing and may live a 1,000 years. All Irish yews are female, and their needles curve. Longbows of yew made English archers the long range artillery of medieval wars. The dark leaves and red berries are poisonous; they are typically grown in enclosed yards and churchyards so that animals cannot eat them. The iron rings set into the outside of the road wall were hitching rings for the horses and donkeys of churchgoers.

Immediately past the school, there are outcrops of rock covered in gorse and heather. There is hazel on the waterside, and birch and goat willow, all once used for making brooms, baskets and lobster pots. In Irish lore, hazels, with their silver and gold branches, had magical properties. Yeats' 'Wandering Aengus' says, "I went into a hazel wood/ Because a fire was in my head..." . The low bushes were once coppiced, and harvested for nuts.

On the stream, pond skaters dash about the surface on splayed legs. On sunny days, their feet are reflected and magnified as four smudges on the sandy bottom, uncannily like the paw prints of an invisible, underwater dog.

Most of our common wild trees can be found along this lane, hawthorn, blackthorn and holly, alder, ash, hazel, sycamore and small oaks. A robust growth of crinkly grey-white lichen colonises the 'sceacs' , aka blackthorns. The ground is rocky, with little grazing. Foxgloves thrive on the roadside, and primeval-looking polypody ferns. Stonecrop, red in spring, creeps over the

Little hut, Roaringwater Creek

rocks, with tiny, succulent-type leaves and, later, tiny, star-like flowers.

As the road descends with the stream, we are separated from the water by bracken and impenetrable breaks of self-seeded trees, largely willows. A snowberry bush, an American import gone native, is suddenly found on the road side. Children like to squeeze and pop its aniseed-ball-size, white berries, or shoot them through pea-shooters made from another garden escapee, the insidious hollow-stemmed Japanese knotweed. Often the two grow close to one another, like dockleafs and nettles. There seems no good reason for this - possibly the seeds are brought together by small girls and boys.

Sometimes, the river bank can be accessed. The water rushes over small cataracts and the patterns and colours of the bark of the riverside saplings is beautiful and infinitely varied. In March, the mini-swamps are golden with marsh marigolds. As we come in view of a white house on the corner, the stream gurgles in a deep gully on our left, perhaps roars (hence the name?) when in flood. Bluebells, and a stand of orchid-like blue flowers, called bugles, speckle the verge. Lime-green hart's tongue ferns - slim and curling as a deer's tongue - grow in the shadows.

A road rises steeply to the right as we reach the gable of the white house; we pass it and cross the small bridge. In a flower bed at the house gable, St Patrick's Cabbage, a Lusitanian species, grows robustly. Lusitanian flora, centred on north west Spain (Lusitania, the ancient name for Iberia), is a phenomenon of Ireland's western seaboard. It includes arbutus, or strawberry tree, pale butterwort, Irish spurge, etc., all of which likely arrived via a land bridge, long since drowned, from Iberia to Britain and Ireland. Fifteen plant species unknown in Britain survive on our mild west coast, especially in West Cork and Kerry. There is also the lusitanian Kerry Slug, found in the south west, its nearest relatives being in Portugal.

St Patrick's Cabbage is a saxifrage and bears no resemblance to the vegetable that goes so well with bacon. The serrated leaves are fat, and tough, arranged in a rosette around the base of the flower stem which shoots to four inches and bears small white flowers in May. On the bridge wall opposite, wild strawberry may be found, both barren strawberry and the variety that carries small, sweet fruits.

A short distance after the bridge, we bear right, following the river as it becomes a tidal creek. Seaweed is in evidence just below the bridge, and large mullet swim up to this point from the sea. Local people tell me otters are regularly seen. The tree-hung bank on the other side would give plenty of cover.

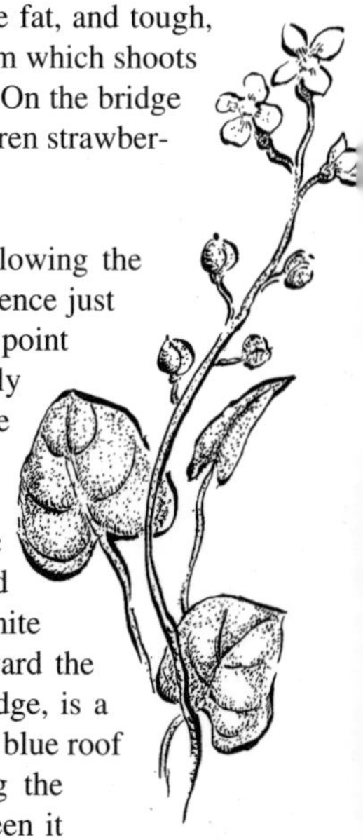

(2) As we round the corner, we come on an idyllic scene, a wide pool of still, brown water, with an old stone quay splashed with the colours of sea pinks, white scurvy grass and the odd prawn pot in spring. Toward the mouth of the inlet, standing alone near the water's edge, is a small, neat corrugated-iron cabin, painted rose, with a blue roof and an object like an inverted cooking pot capping the stovepipe chimney. In April, sea pinks flower between it and the water, and the escarpment behind is bright with gorse. To one side is a stone well, and a track that leads back to the mouths of some small caves in the hillside. The cabin is often occupied by a German scholar, rarely seen, whose many interests include sketching Stone Age sites, drawing West Cork wild mushrooms and exploring connections between the myths of Siegfried (of Mozart's opera) and the progress of the stars. In the tiny interior, all necessities for life and work are at hand. The tenant might well be a latter-day Thoreau, this creek his Walden Pond.

Common scurvy grass

In the past, islanders would have landed at the quay to go to mass, trudging uphill to the church, now in ruins, above the creek. It is worth while dawdling here for a few minutes. Besides the peace, there is much of interest. Various seaweeds cling to the stone ramparts or grow in the water below, channelled wrack, horned wrack and 'egg wrack', as knotted wrack is sometimes called. The latter can be over a metre long, with leathery branches and egg-shaped air bladders. When it's cast up and dries - as it is here - children enjoy stamping on it. A trawl of these weeds with a stout shrimping net will discover crabs, prawns, sea sticklebacks, pretty two-spot gobies and wonderfully ugly but harmless scorpion fish.

Lovely gardens of discreet houses come down to the quay, one with a magnificent Chilean fire tree, flowering like a giant orange fuschia in spring. Wild turnip, a big plant of waste ground, grows in profusion. Ravens nest in the trees opposite and can be heard to squawk. Stately herons stalk the shore below the cabin. Swans, reflected in the brown water, drift to the quays hoping to be fed. Sheldduck, a very beautiful large duck, white, with a striking green-black head, red bill, and chestnut band about the breast, also visit. Unusually, the females are dressed as brightly as the males. Because they nest in old rabbit burrows, their plumage doesn't have to be sod-brown for camouflage, as with mallard, teal and other ducks. This is a lovely corner for wildlife. We have seen a stoat, and various butterflies, including holly blues, painted ladies and, later in the year, red admirals.

Roaringwater, last bridge before the sea

We retrace our steps to the house by the bridge. In its gardens, sloping down to the river, ti trees, (Cordyline Australis) flourish. Known locally as "palms", they are natives of Asia and the Pacific isles. They do well in West Cork's Gulf Stream climate, especially near the sea, where there is rarely frost.

Rounding the gable of the house, we take the road ascending steeply behind it. It's a pretty, leafy road, with a ruined house above it on the right. The climb is short. Celandine, germander speedwell - like forget-me-not - primroses, violets and hedge parsnip throng the verges, each in its season. Honeysuckle festoons the trees. There are fine stands of yellow flag irises right and left, flamboyant flowers of wet ground, blooming in May. We pass the entrance to a house with a long, well-kept lawn, then a vernacular farmhouse and outbuildings with a very vernacular manure-heap in the yard.

Almost at the top of the climb, we find, on the left, an ancient graveyard in which stands the remains of Kilcoe's 18th century RC church, a single gable, and a few graves marked by Celtic crosses. Kilcoe was - and, I'm sure, still is - a very devout parish. We pass three churches on this walk, two ruins and one standing, spanning 500 years. The ancient church wall is a veritable rock garden, colonised by spleenwort, navelwort, stonecrop, vetches and hard ferns.

(3) We top the rise 50 yards along. Mount Gabriel stands dramatically on the skyline. Soon we reach a 4-cross roads, and have two options.

Option (A) we turn sharp left. This takes us to a fine view of Kilcoe Castle and to ancient Kilcoe church and graveyard. The diversion adds $1^{1}/_{2}$ miles to our walk. Afterwards, we return to this cross, and take up the route outlined in Option (B), for which we would now turn sharp right, inland, pursing the 'main' route.

Option (A) Turning sharp left, we follow the road, ignoring turnings into fields. We shortly see the sea to the west, with Mount Gabriel in the mid-distance. From here, the twin orbs on its summit - like giant golf balls or domes on mosques - are in silhouette against the sky, part of a communications system monitoring air and sea traffic on the North Atlantic. Ballydehob Harbour is seen to the east, with the surface of the near sea lined with mussel 'ropes', a recent phenomena. Mussels are 'seeded' onto these.

Kilcoe's 18th century RC church

Kilcole graveyard

They grow quickly, by pumping up to 100 litres of water a day through their gills and extracting minute plankton. When they reach edible size, they are harvested. While farming the sea, rather than ravishing it, seems laudable, local aesthetes and nature lovers say the mussel ropes take from the bay's wildness and grandeur. Others predict disaster for the bay's ecology, fearing that the detritus from millions of mussels will suffocate all bottom-dwelling life. Across the water to the south east, we can see Ringcoliskey Castle on Turk Head, built in 1495, a one-time stronghold of the O'Driscolls. The beacon at Baltimore can be seen in the distance, beyond.

The road divides like a Y; we take the left fork and, descending, enjoy close-up views of Roaringwater Bay. Between us and Reen Point, on our right, we see the twin islets, Illaunroemore and Illaunroebeg (red island big, and small). Cattle graze on the "beg". Now, the huge bay and its islands are laid out in front of us, the surface etched with hundreds of mussel lines.

At the time of writing, cranes and scaffolding surrounded Kilcoe Castle, a fortified tower house of the McCarthy Riabachs, now the property of the actor, Jeremy Irons. After the Battle of Kinsale, 1601, when the victorious English came west to root out the last rebel Irish, Kilcoe withstood a prolonged siege by Lord Carew. Offered escape by sea, its defenders refused and held out into 1603, when it was the last castle in West Cork to surrender. The main tower is of four storeys, the corner tower of six, with dungeons beneath. Built on Mannin Island Beg, now reached by a bridge, it overlooks the larger Mannin island. Mr Irons has spent a fortune on appropriate restoration. It is a unique dwelling in an idyllic spot. The road leading to it is private, but we can enjoy a good view from the road above.

At the end of this road, we reach the graveyard and ruined church of Kilcoe. We pass breaks of flowering currant en route, a garden escapee that brightens the hedges of West Cork with pink flowers. Kilcoe church was already in ruins by 1615. The stone windows are elegant and beautiful, overlooking a rugged and beautiful view. Ruined walls enclose the burial ground, with lines of low, uninscribed gravestones, weathered and lichen-grown. Inscribed headstones and chest tombs date from the 1860s. Overlooking the bay and islands, few resting places can be as sublime as Kilcoe.

We retrace our steps to the cross roads. Sometimes, in spring, a 'fall' of swallows may suddenly come in off the sea. Irish swallows favour Malawi for their winter break; British and continental swallows go elsewhere. Swallows are 'site faithful' and find their way back to the barns or eaves where they were reared.

(4) We arrive at the cross-roads, where we earlier turned left to take up this option. Now, we go straight ahead, inland towards the hills, joining the (B) route.

East window of pre-1615 church at Kilcoe

Option (B). After turning right at the cross-roads, the roadside fields are scrubby, with gorse and rough gazing. At Kilcoe Cross Roads, we cross the main N71 - a good view of Ballydehob Bay to the left - and continue up the small road opposite. After passing a timber yard, there is a neat Church of Ireland graveyard. A cut stone vault of the Townsend family - Castletownshend connections? - is just inside, sealed with a tight-fitting iron door upon which roost dozens of 'petite gris', or common garden snails. These are edible, but never eaten by the Irish. I've seen tortoiseshell butterflies sunning themselves on the door in April, early for them to be abroad. Fine Scots pines edge the site, with singing blackbirds and thrushes on spring evenings.

The road rises and falls in gentle dips. One rarely meets a car. This is a mellow West Cork walk, the quiet road, the bogland, the distant hills, transition from usable land to land that hasn't been changed and is unlikely to ever be. Knockaphukeen (the fairies' mountain) is almost straight ahead, Mount Gabriel and Mount Corrin off to our left. Topping a rise, we look out on

miles of empty hills. A section of the Sheep's Head Way, through Barngeehy (the windy gap), is only a few miles north.
We ignore a road to our left and pass Lisheenacrehig, a few farmhouses by the road side. Once, as we walked the route in May, a conference of magpies festooned the local trees; after counting forty, I gave up. The green fields begin to give way to rock. Irish spurge, with vivid lemon flowers that look like leaves, blooms everywhere hereabouts in May. The seeds of spurge produce an oil sac which ants find irresistible and carry far and wide, eating the sacs and leaving the seeds to take root. Cuckoo flowers grow where the verge is wet; delicate white stichwort hangs from the ditches. Now relatively close to Mount Gabriel, we can see the scars of the ancient copper mines. Reaching the 'T' junction, we take a very sharp right, doubling back towards the sea.

(5) The woodland skirting the road is silver birch and willow. Birch has been in Ireland since the end of the last Ice Age, one of the first colonisers. Once, in early October, I found two fine, largely unwormed birch boletus mushrooms under these trees, with caps big and fat as half jaffa oranges. There may also be saffron milk caps, another good eating mushroom, under the pines - many fungus are symbiotic with certain trees. Some bee hives have been sited at the forest edge; presumably gorse, heather, meadowsweet and, possibly, the catkins of birch and willow provide nectar for the bees.

These seemingly barren uplands are host to many butterflies and moths whose caterpillars feed on bog myrtle, whortleberry and bell heather. 'Hairy Mollies' and the furry caterpillars of fox moths cross the road. Their pretty hairs are defensive, deterring predators by sticking in their eyes.

Between rock outcrops, small 'rivers' of grazing grass are vivid green. In boggy places, willows and rushes grow, and tall royal ferns. Bog cotton, with flower heads like white pennants or bunny tails, speckles the fields. Chiffchaffs flit amongst roadside willows, with the occasional robin or wren. Cock stonechats, with black head, russet breast and white collar, perch on high brambles and sing. I spied a pied flycatcher in May, a blithe newcomer probably en route to inland pastures.

Soon, we reach the N71 again. Turning left, we pass a one-time country post office-shop and - unless we are thirsty - the Cross House Lounge Bar. Only a hundred yards away are the bridge and church where we began.

Rossbrin Harbour and Stouke

Sheltered Rossbrin harbour and quay - Rossbrin Castle - high roads with distant views of Baltimore and beacon - Stouke Burial Ground - panorama of Roaring Water Bay and the islands.

Locality: OS Sheet 88 starting in square 9731, south of the Ballydehob-Schull road, about 2$^1/_2$ miles west of Ballydehob.

Description and Distance: A loop walk taking us from the sea inland towards the hills, and back to the sea. Two options, (A) 3 miles and (B) 4$^1/_2$ miles.

Walking Time: 2 or 3 hours, allowing time for the views and the wayside attractions. Country lanes with little traffic. One short, steep climb.

Features: The quiet harbour at Rossbrin is a lovely spot, the surface often still as a lake, with the O'Mahony castle on the headland opposite reflected on the water. As we walk inland, we have views east as far as Baltimore, west as far as Schull. The option, slightly longer, takes us to historic Stouke graveyard. Roaringwater Bay and the islands are laid out below us as we gently descend back to the sea.

Flora and fauna: Seals, mullet and sea birds in the harbour. Seaweeds and shells. Shoreline plants and wild flowers. Upland gorse, fuschia and heather. Rabbits, sometimes hares.

Equipment: Ordinary walking shoes.

Itinerary:

(1) We set off from Rossbrin Quay, reached, most simply, by taking a left turn off the Ballydehob to Schull Road, the R592, signposted Rossbrin Cove.

The cove was once a busy place, when copper mines in the hinterland used the quay to ship out ore, and islanders used it as a landfall, taking produce to market and children to school.

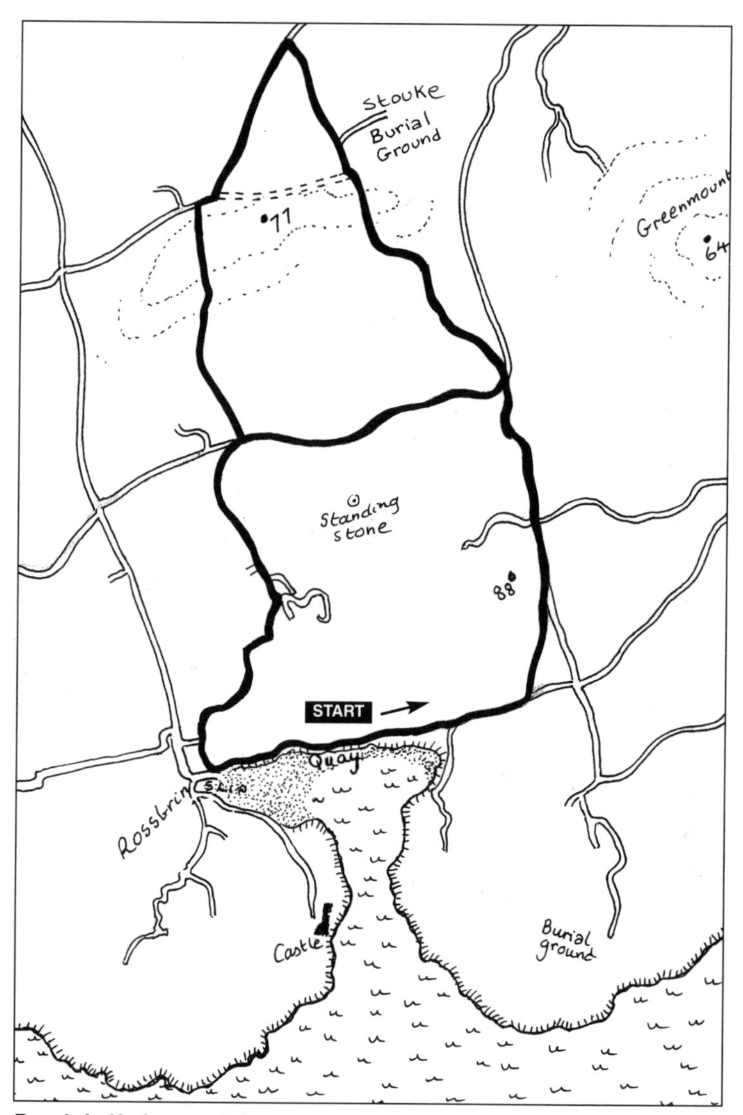

Rossbrin Harbour and Stouke

Having walked the route in winter and summer, I set out to record it one lovely spring evening. Immediately I parked the car at the quay, I saw what looked like a black net float shining on the flat-calm water about fifty yards from shore. When it suddenly disappeared, I realised it was a seal. A few moments later, it resurfaced, a female or immature grey - much smaller than an adult male - with the grey's distinctive sloped forehead. The water was no more than six foot deep and when she dived, one could clearly follow her progress underwater. Mullet swirled and jumped in the shallows as she approached. She appeared again near the old slip, in front of the boatyard.

For a minute at a time, between bird song, silence hung over the inlet. With its narrow mouth, it is like a lake. The ruined tower of the O'Mahony castle on the opposite headland was perfectly reflected in the water, the image reaching half way to the shore where I stood. The month was April, almost May, the weather mild - a 'pet day', as they say in West Cork.

The O'Mahony castle, Rossbrin Castle, a rectangular tower on a rock outcrop at the west side of Rossbrin Bay, was reputedly built in 1310, but the surviving remains are of 15th or 16th century origin. Once a centre of learning under Finghin O'Mahony, "the scholar prince of Rossbrin", it was abandoned in the early 17th century, after the Irish-Spanish defeat at the Battle of Kinsale. The remains stand to four storeys on the north east corner, like a finger pointing at the sky. It is a romantic ruin, in a perfect setting and is seen from many perspectives on this walk. The O'Mahonys won much land from the once more powerful O'Driscolls. Other O'Mahony castles are at Three Castle Head, Leamcon, Ardintenant, Dunmanus and Dunbeacon. O'Driscoll castles are on the islands, Sherkin and Cape Clear. There is a McCarthy castle at Kilcoe, now the property of the actor, Jeremy Irons (Roaringwater Bay Walk).

Local lore tells us that in a field behind the cove, known as the "Palaces", there was a 'fish palace', producing 'trayn oil' (nothing to do with locomotives). During the halcyon fishing years of the 17th and 18th centuries, pilchards, a small, oily fish, shoaled in millions along these shores. No trace remains of the building or the shoals. Fish palaces were a distinctive West Cork phenomenon of those days.

Sea pinks sprout from fissures between the stone blocks of the pier, and scurvy grass, with small white flowers, grows in mats along the edge. How

Rossbrin, wreck, ruin, and heron

convenient, that it grew so close to the sea, this important source of vitamin C for old-time sailors facing long voyages and scurvy which, at best, merely rotted their gums, at worst, took their lives.

Sea weeds, in long trails, float on the surface, buoyed by their 'bubbles', which carry the fronds up to the light as the tide rises. Knotted wrack is most common but spiral and channelled wrack grows in abundance. These shallow water algaes are an ideal habitat for 6 inch long, fifteen spined 'sea' sticklebacks. Rarely seen but easy to catch with a net, they are best not disturbed in summer, when 'nesting'. Like their freshwater cousins, the male is nest builder, housekeeper, baby sitter and 'minder', keeping the females from eating the young.

A wrecked boat lies beside the pier, overgrown with weed. As we make our way east along the water - the sea on our right - bluebells grow on the verge in spring. A few lovely houses are set back from the road, fronted by gracious lawns. Outside them are clumps of libertia, a New Zealand flower, their tall spears covered in white flowers. Between us and the water, small fuschias and whitethorns edge the lane. The dark green grass is peppered with white stitchworth. The water reflects the old stone walls, dappled with orange lichen, that edge the eastern shore.

Ransoms - 'wild garlic' - grows in profusion before we come to the small pebble beach at the eastern end, its oniony odour distinctive as we pass. In May, it is a lovely sight on Irish roadsides, with three-cornered stems and white flowers. However, farmers fear it - if cows eat it, it taints the milk.

In the field ahead, red-brown rabbits hop about on summer evenings, a black rabbit amongst them (unless it was a cat - but even in this peaceful kingdom, it is unlikely that nature would have cats playing with rabbits).
A small, gurgling stream pours from the under the honeysuckle on a ditch on our left. The pebble beach is worth ten minutes. For the children, there is much dried 'egg' wrack to pop. The rocks are splattered with orange lichen, bright as the yolk of sea gull eggs. Pinks, scurvy grass and large, glossy-leafed sea beet grows here, the latter, a relative of beetroot and sugar beet, is one of the few plants that can survive salt spray. It was eaten with bacon and pork in times past.

Curlew Rossbrin

Amongst other specialist plants of the sea shore, moss campion and rock sea spurrey roots on nearby walls and rocks. The lapidary volume on the botany of the islands of Roaring Water Bay, "The Wild Plants of Sherkin and Cape Clear and adjacent islands" published by the Marine Station on Sherkin, mentions spurrey and campions as present on the islands offshore.

As we leave the sea, a gate on our right is imaginatively and patriotically decorated with metal net balls atop metal pillars, the whole painted green, white and yellow, Ireland's colours, slightly fading and rusting in the salt air.

Spurge grows profusely on the roadside, with pines on the left, and gunnera, giant 'wild rhubarb', outside a house. The road climbs now, grass growing down the middle. We take the first left (where "32" is printed on the OS map). The climb, for a few hundred yards, is quite steep. Behind us, are marvellous views, Rossbrin Castle, and Castle Island behind it, with the gables of ruined houses against the sky. Other islands are the Calf group, low on the sea.

At the top of this stretch, Baltimore Harbour comes into view to the east, with the white beacon opposite Sherkin Pier shining in the sun. We are on a

Rossbrin, scurvygass, sea pink and sea beet

small back road, now, a dusty bohreen in summer. A road merges from the right. Gorse and heather come down to the road side. We top a rise and, as we pass a 'cross-roads' (the left junction, a cattle grid, with big gates, leads only to a farm) we are going down, heading towards the rolling hills in the distance. Foxgloves grow along the ditch, reaching almost two metres tall in good years. The fields are scrubby, with white reeds in the lowland bogs. The green of grass, the white of reeds, the gold of gorse are like an Irish tri-colour laid across the land.

(2) We now come to a 4-cross roads, (where the latitude "33" is printed on the OS map), and have two options.

Option (A) takes us to Stouke Burial Ground, adding 1½ miles to the walk.
Option (B) takes a shorter loop back to base.

Option (A) We go straight through the cross roads, taking the small road going north west, keeping to the higher land.

On the left, we immediately pass a large rock in a field, with ivy growing up it from a single, thick stem, splaying out, like a one dimensional tree. The road climbs higher, a quiet road, grass growing up the middle. Now, we have a wonderful view of Mount Gabriel, the twin "golf balls" of the communications stations on top. In spring, the hedge of berberis outside a house on our right is dark green, with prickly, holly-like leaves and little orange flowers, contrasting with the robust yellow gorse growing through it.

The road rises, at times as if making straight for Mount Gabriel, four miles away. Reaching a 'summit', it starts downhill. Shortly, we find the Burial Ground on our right, a small gate, freshly painted blue at the time of writing. Inside, are old graves, especially towards the back, many of them unmarked. There is a bullaun stone in the south east corner. Bullaun stones may have been primitive mortars for grinding grain or baptismal fonts at ancient churches, where they are often found. Often, legend ascribes magic properties to the water that settles in the scooped cup of the stone, that it rises and falls with the tides, that it is effective in curing warts. The grave yard is still in occasional use, indeed when the illustrator of this book went to sketch it, she found a gravedigger with a newly unearthed skull. He was digging a grave for a man from Cork and said it was not unusual to accidentally expose the bones of earlier occupants. An impressive rhododendron thrives near the back wall.

Leaving the graveyard, we continue our route. The road to the left, marked on the map, now passes through the farmyard of a fine, two storey farmhouse. The owner may allow walkers through, if asked. Otherwise, we continue and take the next left, walking two sides of the triangle rather than one, but they are not very long.

This left turn is finger posted "Stouke Stud", and there is immediately a house on the right with the legend, "Upper Crust Bakery" on the gable. We might pause to marvel at Irish rural industry, a bakery in this incongrous setting. Alongside this upland road, furze blooms in the small fields of rough grazing. In spring, linnets, small brown birds, the male with a russet forehead and breast, sing as we pass.

At the first T junction, we turn right and, a hundred yard along, take the road left, making south for the sea. The road descends and we come to a 4-cross roads. Options (A) and (B) now merge. We go straight across, taking the road sign-posted "Riding School".

Option (B) We turn sharp left at the cross-roads, almost going back on ourselves, on a road slightly higher than the one we are on. It winds uphill. The fields ahead are on two levels, like grassy terraces. We are soon on a sort of plateau, with rocky outcrops to the left and the twin domes atop Mount Gabriel dead ahead, perhaps four miles away. To our right, are wide views over rough land, dotted with grazing cattle. The OS map shows two 'broken line' paths to the left, and a ring fort between them. The paths are not obvious and permission may be necessary to enter the land. The bohreen we are walking on is quiet and pleasant and we keep to it, continuing to the cross roads.

At the cross-roads, the Options merge as the longer, Stouke Burial Ground loop, (A), joins us from the right. We turn left, down the road finger-posted "Riding School".

(3) In March, the low-growing, pretty yellow flowers of the lesser celandine are common on the roadside followed, in April and May, by goldilocks and meadow buttercups growing very tall to clear the grasses when they flower. Celandine is the first of the spring flowers and possibly the best known. The shiny golden heads have pointed petals; those of the buttercup are rounded. The leaves of the buttercup are 'ragged', those of the celandine are like small, shiny, dark green hearts. Wordsworth, whom the poet Ezra Pound described as a "silly old sheep with a genius", was a fan of the celandine, devoting a whole poem to it, marvelling at its habit of closing when clouds come over and opening "....Bright as the sun himself" when the clouds pass. Indeed, the small, yellow faces of the flowers, with their spiky petals, resemble children's drawings of the sun.

The road, given occasional humps and dips, is descending to the sea. On one low rise, we pass some old, white-washed farm buildings. The riding school is up a track to the left. We follow the road right, and come out on breathtaking views over Horse Island, then Castle Island, with its castle down by the water. A channel separates them, with the low-lying Dereen Rocks between.

The road descends steeply, the O'Mahony castle is straight ahead. Our route hairpins around to the right and here, indeed, is a 'photo opportunity'; one cannot but be taken by the view. On nearby Horse Island, we can clearly see the pier and old grey houses blending perfectly into the landscape. Beyond, are the 'outer islands', and beyond them, the great bulk of Oileán Cléire, Irish-speaking Cape Clear Island, the highest - some say the biggest, notwithstanding Sherkin - in Roaringwater Bay.

Before the Famine of 1845, Cape Clear's population was 1,200; it is now 150. Each family was self-supporting, the men ploughing the sea, the women ploughing the land. Every arable inch was tilled, sheep raised, oats and barley grown and milled. A Neolithic passage tomb, perhaps 6,000 years old, was recently found on the highest hill; patently, boats must have been used by early Irish man. St. Ciarán's church, now in ruins near the pier, is said to have been the first Christian church in Ireland. Dún an Óir is the remains of an impressive O'Driscoll castle. Cape Clear is charming and peaceful, another world, set in another time.

The lane we walk is leafy and pleasant. We pass a big red barn on our left, and some very nice whitewashed stone buildings, with red tin roofs. In a field to our right, are two stone-built pillars, like massive gateposts, the remains of old quarry workings. On the right, are tall grasses - libertia, again, with white flowers. In April, wild bluebells skirt this road.

Across a field, on the 'main' road, we see the old National School, painted

The old Rossbrin school

pink. Built in 1909, it served locals and islanders until it was closed in the 1960s. We come to a 'Road narrows' sign, and a sign indicating a snaking piece of road. Now, back at sea level, we round a stone wall and pass between two quaint old buildings, one on either side of the road. One was a shop for the islanders, run by an old lady who died, aged 90, only a few years ago. To our right, is the old boat slip, with a low, rusted barge which has decayed into it, seemingly melding with the stone. The boatyard behind us was started in 1993 by a German couple, dry docking pleasure craft - as many as 80 - in winter, and carrying out maintenance and repairs.

From here, the quay where we began is just a few minutes along the water-side. It is always tempting to linger awhile on the pier before leaving. Rossbrin is a hard spot to leave.

Letter and Barnancleeve Gap

The hills above Schull - an old 'green' road - silence and solitude - bog hole life - prehistoric copper mines - magnificent views.

Locality: OS Sheet 88, starting at square 9534, about 2 miles north of Schull. The starting point can most easily be reached by turning north, towards the hills, off the main Ballydehob to Schull road, approximately half way between the two towns. The turning is signposted "Derryconnell House" and "Schull Deep Sea Angling Centre". Pass Derryconnell House. The road turns sharp left soon afterwards. Ignore the entrance to a house on the right and continue to a small cottage on the right, hidden behind an escalonia hedge, with a chimney with two pots, the 'last' house on the road. Just beyond its gable is a gate and a green roadway leading to the hills. We set out from here.

Description and Distance: A loop walk of about 5 miles, on a green road or little used by-roads.

Walking Time: 2 to 3 hours.

Walking conditions: 20% off road, on an old track. This can be muddy in winter. A gradient, for a short distance, but no steep climbs.

Features: Truly getting away from it all, this circuit has all the qualities of a hill walk, without the long hauls or dizzy raptures. One is unlikely to meet another soul, especially on the green stretch. Hill top views are 360°, with a magnificent panorama of Roaringwater Bay and the islands from Barnancleeve Gap.

Flora and fauna: Montane and sub montane vegetation - western 'dwarf' gorse, and heather, bogs and frogs, sedges and bog myrtle. Roadside stands of foxgloves, some fuschia hedges. Ravens, pipits, larks and stonechats are par for this route, pheasants also, and sometimes a merlin, a small, fleet hawk, may be seen. A good chance of hearing the cuckoo in Spring.

Equipment: Stout, waterproof footwear in winter. Walking shoes at other times

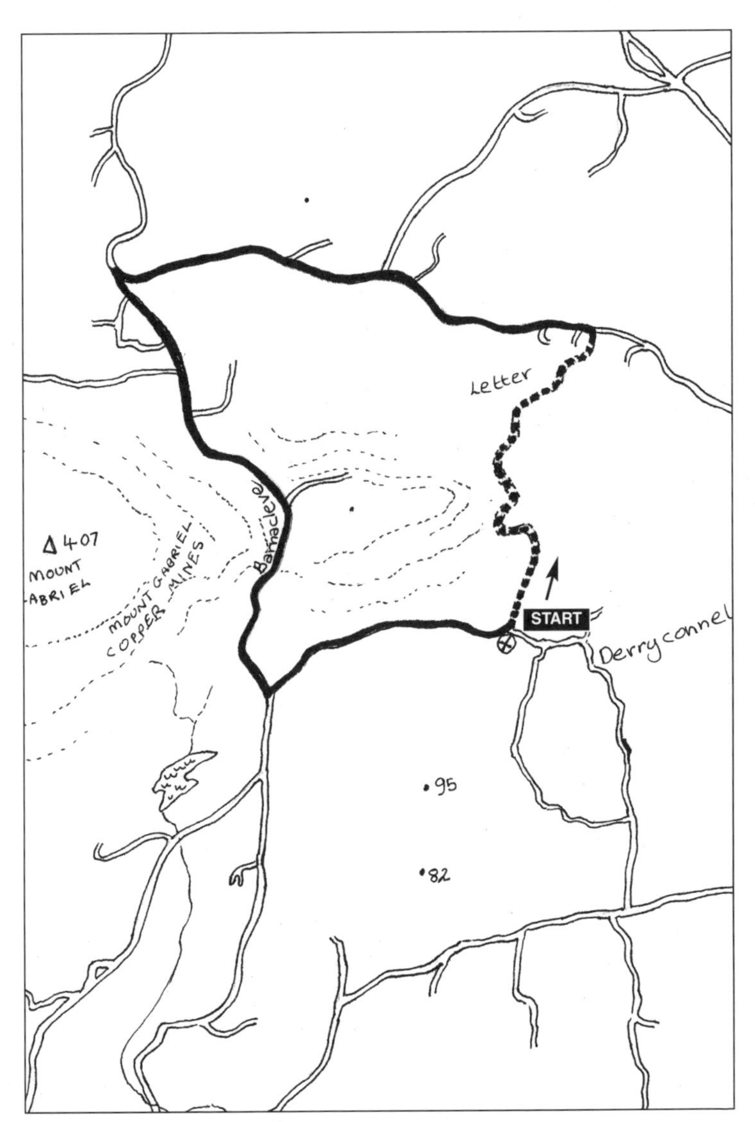

Letter and Barnancleeve Gap

Itinerary

(1) The green road on which we set out for Letter - 'leitir', meaning 'wet hillside' - has a gate at the entrance. We will encounter three gates on this route. Care should be taken to ensure that they are left as found; cattle and sheep graze the rough land in between, and the gates are there for a purpose. Also, walkers should take care to avoid the animals, especially when there are calves or lambs, and to keep dogs well in control.

This path is probably very old. It leads from nowhere to nowhere now but once there was a hill fort on the west side, and the name was 'Leitir an Lis', 'hillside of the fort'. There were ancient copper and barytes mines close by, and the shafts can still be found. A red circle signifying a ring fort is marked on the OS map. However, the path, traced by a broken line, is virtually impassable. When we tried, we ended up in a bog with a bull which, happily, was more interested in a cow.

If you walk this route in May, listen for the cuckoo. Christine Thery, who illustrated this book, was talking to the old man at the 'last' house on a lovely May morning when the cuckoo's notes rang out clear across the hills. He said it had come in late April, the same time as it was first heard near Christine's home, Heir Island, in Roaringwater Bay. The cuckoo will, hereabouts, likely be seeking meadow pipits as surrogates, and the eggs the female cuckoo lays will resemble the pipit's in colour, if not in size. Cuckoos' eggs roughly 'match' those of the host species - so there are meadow pipit cuckoos, wagtail cuckoos, reed warbler cuckoos and so on. The hen cuckoo lays from 8 to 18 eggs in May and June. Only the male sings 'cuckoo'; the female chuckles, perhaps because evolution has relieved her of housekeeping.

As we walk between the flat fields of rough grazing, the silence is, at once, noticeable. One may hear the harsh croak of a raven, or the thrill of a lark high above. Larks are easily identified by their habit of climbing the sky so high as to almost disappear from sight and, circling there, filling the air with song. The song may be sustained as long as five minutes, continuing as they come back to earth. They are ground nesters, building under a hummock of grass. As children, we found it easy to discover their nests simply by watching where they landed. Nowadays, larks are in short supply everywhere. A century ago, boxes of fresh lark tongues arrived at city markets each morning. Thought to have aphrodisiac qualities, many recipe books described their preparation. However, the principal reason for their disappearance is loss of habitat, old long grass meadows being nowadays subsumed beneath silage grass prairies.

Ravens are holding their own, at least in West Cork where they are fairly common, nesting in coastal and inland cliffs, and tree hollows. The largest of our crows, they are slightly bigger than rooks from which they are distinguished by their heavy, all-black bill and glossy plumage. Their guttural croak seems especially loud amongst these silent hills, where the bones of sheep, picked clean and bleached by weather, are testament to the scavenging role of ravens in this environment.

Cow, magpie and the back of Mt. Gabriel, Barnancleve gap

We cross a brown stream at another gate. The surface, and that of most bog pools we will encounter, is often alive with whirligig beetles and pond skaters. When water meets air, a film is formed, and these insects totally rely upon its properties for habitat and food. Small flies and insects are their prey; for these, the surface is like glue and they cannot escape it once they alight. Just as a spider feels the struggles of a fly in its web, the whirligigs and skaters sense the struggles of the insect via the surface membrane. Try drumming lightly on the surface with the tip of a bog rush. Beetles will whizz or skate across the surface to it, expecting a captive lunch.

Foxgloves grow along the edge of the stream, a tall, impressive plant with many flowers like purple finger-stalls, much frequented by bumble bees. A few blackthorn bushes grow nearby in this tree-less landscape, one covered with ivy; hundreds of drone flies and hover flies feed on the green ivy buds in the sun, setting up a melodious hum when disturbed.

The path swings left and then right and climbs gently. Roaringwater Bay, behind us, can now be seen, and Cape Clear Island. As we climb, the Fastnet Rock, ten miles due south, is visible and, to the south east, the beacon at Baltimore, and Baltimore village itself, famous for its sailing club and

Algerian pirates. Gorse bushes, the spiky limbs so thick with flower that they look like yellow bottle brushes, brighten the hill side. Gorse - also known as furze or whins - blooms all year, although less so in winter. This habit inspired a cute old saw to the effect that "Kissing is out of season when gorse is out of bloom... " Western gorse, a smaller variety, and bell heather blankets the ground between rock outcrops, making diversions from the path a prickly business.

Besides whirligigs, the bog holes support lesser water boatmen, which swim on top and scavenge on the bottom. Their cousins, the greater water boatmen, swim upside down and have a vicious beak to which I can attest, having once handled one and been savaged. Greater water boatmen will prey on tadpoles which may be found hereabouts in wayside drains. Unslurried and unsullied, landscapes like this still provide healthy habitat for the common frog.

We reach the highest point of the green road. Ahead of us, the land falls away and then, in the near distance, rises again to hills with brown slopes of bracken, green conifer plantations, and golden breaks of gorse. To the north west, we see the high mountains of Kerry beyond Dunmanus and Bantry Bay. The mountain straight ahead has a cairn of stones on top. Between us and it, the landscape is sparsely populated; there are no more than ten houses, some hidden by trees. As the old road decends, Mount Gabriel is to our extreme left, high above.

We reach the first few trees, hawthorns and blackthorns, or 'sceacs', as locally known, a rough word for a tough tree. They are gnarled and wind bent by the prevailing south westerlies. Evidence of the weathering effect of these winds can be seen where the rock outcrops are roughly flat on top. Grooves run in a north easterly direction across the surface, all parallel, made by rain drops driven by the south west wind.

(2) There are ruins of stone houses on the left, and a copse of trees ahead. We arrive at the third and last gate, a serious barrier. Once, the farmers in the

Cuckoo with meadow pipit 'mother'

house just beyond kindly offered to help me move it back into position after I passed through. Here is a case where the amenity value of this green roadway should be developed by the local authority, and a stile installed.

After the exit gate, we pass a large, neat farmhouse on the right and, to the left, there are old buildings, the ancient stone walls beautifully patterned with lichens. Now, the road is paved and we pass whitewashed out-houses, with red oxide painted doors and tin roofs, and a nice garden where butterflies flit over the buddleia. An escalonia hedge and then a stone wall, the stones set vertically, in the Irish fashion. Brambles have found a hold, and fuschia; this humble wall supports a diversity of plant species which could while away an hour of investigation. There is tormentil, with red stems and small yellow flowers, maidenhair spleenworth, with tiny leaves like beadlets on either side of the woody stems; there is hard fern, wall rue, buckler fern, harts tongue fern and polypody. Mosses thrive in thick green cushions, wall pennyworth (aka navelworth) sends up stalks of bell shaped flowers like tiny foxgloves.

At the end of the lane, we reach the narrow main road and turn left. In October, the whitethorn bushes are red with shining haws, the blackthorns purple with sloes. Sloes are the wild ancestors of plums but it is wondrous how human ingenuity produced nectar-dripping Victoria plums from the tart, bitter fruit of these mountain sceacs. Masayo Sawasaki, who took photos for these walks, tried one and said it reminded her of a Japanese sour plum, a pickled fruit which I remember as one of the few Japanese delights I did not enjoy.

Hooded crow at Mount Gabriel

A lone house in the landscape, Letter old road.

We pass red barns on the left and, some minutes further on, the cottage of the respected poet, John Montague, more often teaching at American universities than at home. It is certainly a poetic location, with peace in abundance and wild, stark scenery. Montague's lines in his poem 'King & Queen', "...band after band/ of terminal,/ peewit haunted/ cropless bogland." might have been written about this landscape but hereabouts the lapwing is called the 'pilibín' rather than the 'peewit'. Both names echo its lonely cry, while 'lap-wing' perhaps refers to the slow beat of its rounded wings.

We are now walking due west; Mount Gabriel is, at times, dead ahead. A stream a few yards wide crosses under the road; willow and alder grow along it. Alder is typical along most Irish watercourses, a tree which although deciduous, has evolved a small 'cone' . This falls and floats downstream and seeds along the banks. It is a 'pioneer species' in wet and marginal lands, capable of fixing atmospheric nitrogen in the soil and thus improving it. Siskins, pretty, yellow finches, often feast on alder catkins in winter, hanging upside down as they feed.

We ignore a road to the right, going north. Bogland is to our left, and also to our right, at times. Tussock sedge and soft rush grows in the wet places; where there is rock showing, bell heather and western dwarf gorse often colonies the fissures. The road is straight, and treeless - although there are the usual small willows, and bog myrtle - a hot road on a warm day.

(3) Arriving at a T-junction, the main Schull-Durrus road, we turn left. . There is a house on our right, with some leylandi trees and, on the other side of the 'main' road, a house across the field with pines lining the driveway.

As we walk south - climbing gently towards the gap at Barnancleeve - the land below us on the left is trenched and ploughed for forestation. Beyond the rushy fields are views to rolling hills. Fuschia bushes verge the roadside here and there, and on the left are quite a lot a small trees, hazel, blackthorn, white thorn, birch especially. The road continues to rise gently, giving wider and wider views.

The islands of Roaringwater Bay

The cleft between Mount Gabriel and the hill opposite is a small gorge, worn by weather - Barnancleeve, probably from Bearna an Chleibh, a basket shaped gap or defile. As we top the rise, we come upon a spectacular view. The road clings to the Mt. Gabriel side, where the escarpment is steep, as in a 'cutting'. Roaringwater Bay and many of its islands and islets - said to number one hundred - lies spread out below us, an awe-inspiring sight. The largest fully in view is Clear Island, the smallest and most dramatic, the Fastnet Rock.

The Fastnet Rock, Carrig Aoner (the lonely rock) in Irish, has had a beacon since 1853, with the present lighthouse built in 1904. Until 1989, four lighthouse men lived on the rock, where tides rise 12 feet and currents can run dangerously fast. On only a dozen tides a year is the water calm enough to allow a safe landing. In 1979, during the Cowes to Fastnet yacht race (a 5 day voyage) a fierce storm caught competitors between Lands End and Schull. While many lives were saved by the Courtmacsherry, Baltimore and other British and Irish lifeboats, many boats sank and fifteen competitors were drowned. In the past, a fanciful local myth said that on May Day the Fastnet went west to Kerry to meet its relations, The Bull, The Cow and The Calf, islands off the tip of Beara, but that since the lighthouse was built it could no longer do so, being pinned down with steel.

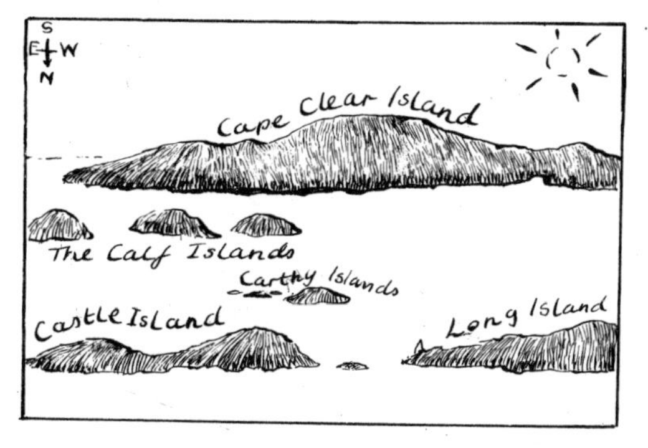

Along the roadside, St Patrick's cabbage, Saxifraga spathularis Brot, a Lusitanian species, grows in a profusion I have not seen elsewhere. From the base of a rosette of leaves, not unlike that of a lawn daisy but tougher, a flower spike rises and bears small white flowers in May. The roadside and the slopes of the gully below are, literally, carpeted in this rare plant, largely confined to West Cork and Kerry, one of fifteen Irish plants that do not grow in Britain.

In the gap, the rock faces are hosts to healthy lichens, an indication of the pure quality of the air. On the west-facing vertical face is a prehistoric copper mine, another at the south end, penetrating some five metres, with an entrance about a metre high. A stone maul - hammer - was found here. Goat willow thrives in the deep water course below the road, . Above it, humps of bare rock 'flow' down the hillside, divided by 'streams' of vegetation and cross hatched with fissures, in which heather and scutch grass grows. Behind us are hills behind hills, the blue hills of Kerry in the distance.

We start downward, the road visible below us almost all the way to Schull. Far off to our left, we can see part of the village of Baltimore, its beacon gleaming white in sunlight, visible to the naked eye on clear days. A variety of butterflies forage on the wild flowers, thistles and fuschia in this upland country; in early spring, I've seen painted ladies from North Africa, peacocks, and tortoiseshells, and many red admirals later in the year. Willows with reddish branches and white downy buds hang over the roadside ditches, in springtime blanketed in whortleberry with globular flowers like small red currants or tiny Chinese-lanterns. The twin 'hump backs' of Clear Island stand large and high six miles out in the bay - a ferry plies to the islands from Schull Pier. Basking sharks, porpoises, dolphins, even migrating whales, are regularly seen in these waters.

In May and June, the road side is purple with foxgloves, beautiful but poisonous flowers, the original source of digitalis, effective in the treatment of heart complaints. 'Digitalis' is named for 'digits', presumably - but children should not stick their fingers in foxgloves because there may be bumble bees inside.

(4) Half a mile or so below the gap, we see pine trees ahead, and a white house with two chimneys. Here, we turn left. There is an old house on the right with a tin roof. On the road outside, I saw a glorious peacock butterfly in early April, flashing its wings as I approached. The 'eyes' on the wings are a defensive device, discouraging predators. Peacocks are less often seen than in yore, the dearth of nettle beds in new, neat farmyards having reduced their numbers. The caterpillars feed on nettles, gluing the leaves into envelopes with small webs, like cocoons.

A fuschia hedge edges the road for a long way, on the right. A house surrounded by trees is called Gabriel's Cottage; it has an attractive wooden garden house. The road is undulating, a lonely road in the fastness of the hills. The fuschia gives out, and there are no ditches or walls on either side, only a few straggling fence posts. Dwarf gorse and bell heather clings to the rocks in the boggy fields, colonised by huge royal ferns, and speckled with the white 'bunny tails' of bog cotton. Pipits fly twittering from rock to rock, and alight, flicking their tails. A raven cries harshly overhead.

It was mid-May when I walked this route in preparation for 'writing' it. Bright yellow tormentil and white cuckoo flowers grew amongst the roadside rushes. As I neared the 'last' house where I began, I, like Christine, heard the cuckoo, and looked for it in the empty hills and bogs around me. With the haunting voice in the distance and the absence of time in the landscape, the earth indeed appeared to be "an insubstantial, faery place" as “the silly old sheep”, aka William Wordsworth put it. The cuckoo’s notes worked magic for Wordworth, and they worked magic for me.

The Old Workhouse and Rathcool

The Old Workhouse - a Bronze Age Stone Row - bog roads - Mount Gabriel - road bowling - 3,000 year old Boulder Burials.

Locality: OS Sheet 88, starting at square 9332, about $^1/_2$ mile east of Schull, on the Ballydehob road. .

Description and Distance: A loop walk of about 3 miles.

Walking Time: 2 hours. Spring and summer are best, for the gorse, heather and fuschia.

Walking conditions: All on quiet back roads, with few, if any cars. No steep climbs.

Features: The old workhouse and hospital. Bronze Age Standing Stones. Then, wild country, with straight and undulating bog roads and Mount Gabriel ahead, scars of the prehistoric copper mines on the slopes, modern day communication 'golf balls' on the summit. On the return route, possibly traditional road "bough-lers" enjoying their unique sport. Panoramic views over Roaringwater Bay and the islands. Boulder burials in a field near the road.

Flora and fauna: Corridors of fuschia, lily ponds, royal ferns, bog plants. Flag irises and whortleberries. Birds of the uplands, ravens, grey crows, meadow pipits and stonechats. Snipe haunt the bogs.

Equipment: Ordinary walking shoes.

Itinerary:

Going east from Schull centre, on the R592, Ballydehob road, we count the left turnings. The first is the turning opposite the Car Park. We continue to the fourth left, about a kilometre distant, where we see a high, ivy grown stone wall on the roadside. The walk begins here, at the corner of the workhouse enclosure.

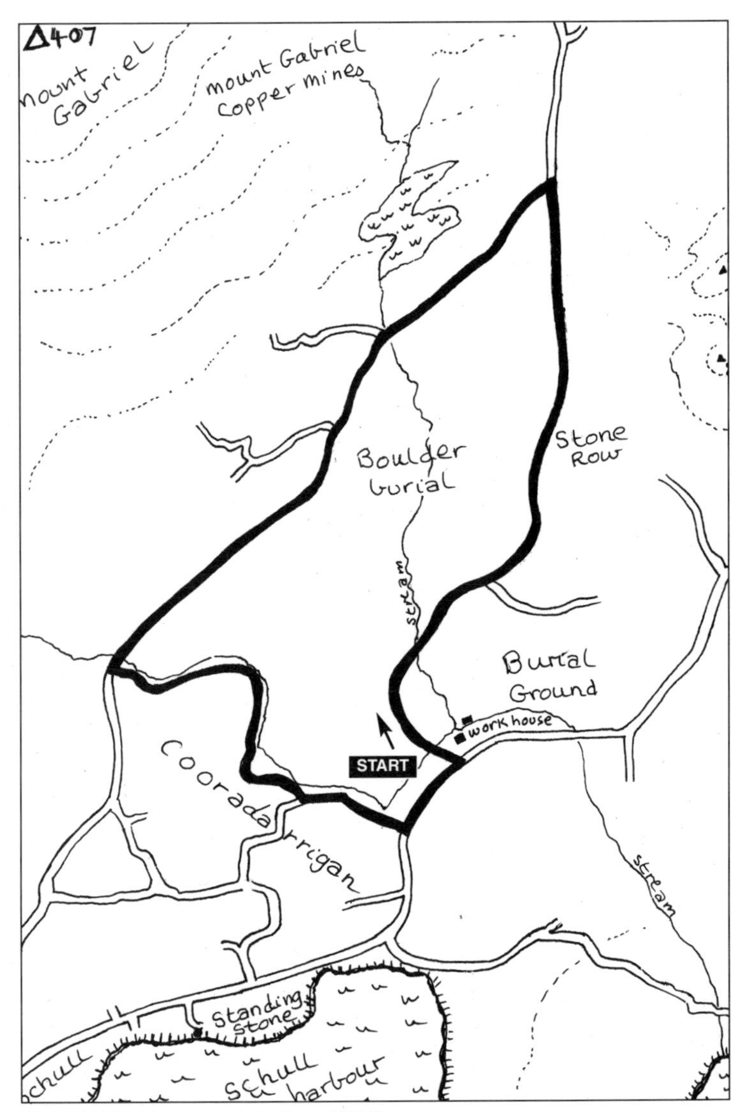

The Old Workhouse and Rathcool Walk

(1) We walk left off the main road, towards the hills. The high stone wall runs for a hundred yards before an opening, barred with an elaborate iron gate overgrown with ivy. Inside, can be seen the ruins of the workhouse and hospital, built to lodge, feed and minister to victims of the Great Famine, 1845 to 1848. Not completed until 1850, it was immediately crowded with destitutes from auxiliary houses in Schull. Many may have stood at this very gate, pleading for admission. The charity of the workhouse was a last option, but many clamoured for entry.

Their fields black with rotting potatoes, their cabins razed because they could not pay rent, the landless Irish, devastated by famine and disease, dragged themselves to the workhouses. "To Clonakilty, God help us!" was a common lament - Clonakilty, another town in West Cork was the site of a charitable institution, its name lost to history. Folk memory records that in Clonakilty and Skibbereen many destitute died in the street outside the workhouse walls for want of space. But admission was often another kind of death sentence. Cholera raged amongst the overcrowded under-fed. Many died in this and other workhouses.

Behind the ruined buildings, was the burial ground. The local Mizen Historical Society has identified 160 uninscribed stones, some possibly marking not single but mass graves. Bodies were carried from the workhouse or hospital out onto the road we stand on, and then around the corner, along a path parallel to the present R592. Thus, the graveyard was not crossed by the funeral cortege but reached from the rear, as was the custom.

Both workhouse and hospital were burnt during the War of Independence, 1916, to prevent their use as barracks by the British Auxiliary Forces, the rapacious Black and Tans.

The wall continues past the gate for a distance, and the road, just wide enough for a car, begins to climb. The sea is behind us and we are walking towards Mount Gabriel, slightly to our left. The road, for three or more hundred yards is a continuous corridor of fuschia, coming into bloom from April onward. It is glorious in mid summer when the purple flowers reflect on the walkers as they pass, or are fallen to make a purple carpet of the road. Yeats, in "Inishfree", talking about "a purple glow" , may have been referring to heather, but the West Cork fuschia hedges - many, now, sacrificed to make wider roads - create an avenue of purple, with a purple world between.

We come over a slight rise and the scenery ahead is mountainous and dramatic, with a deep gap worn in the ridge against the skyline. One might expect a waterfall but it is, in fact, a gap worn out and polished by a glacier, now utilised by the road northward to Durrus, at the head of Dunmanus Bay. The two giant 'golf balls' on the summit - part of a network of communications monitoring air and sea traffic in the North Atlantic - are clearly visible. Celandine, primroses and dog violets splash the green ditches with colour in spring.

West Cork cloudscape

At a corner, a bohreen crosses the road, and there is a graveyard of derelict cars on the right. On the left, clearly visible in a field, are two large upright boulders, these being part of a Stone Row, dating from the Bronze Age and identified on the OS map. A local farmer tells me that, in the field beyond, there was a "poll talún", meaning, literally, "a hole in the ground". The hole usually led to a small complex of underground chambers probably used, as in ring fort farmsteads of the early Christian period, for the storage of foodstuffs and grain. A dog once found its way down and could be heard barking deep underground. The entrance shafts were filled by a farmer some thirty years ago, perhaps even then worried about accidents leading to 'compensation'.

We are soon walking along a bog road, typically undulating, typically dead straight for long stretches. Driving across bog roads is like taking a switchback ride. As children, we kept hoping we'd might meet a good humpbacked bridge and dent the roof of the car with our heads.

Ahead, we can see the hairpin road climbing the side of Mount Gabriel and, above it, a fresh scar in the hillside. This is the site of the most recent excavations of the Bronze Age copper mines. These were worked from 1700BC to 1500 BC, making them the oldest copper diggings in Western Europe. There are thirty two mining sites on the mountain. A number of ancient tools have been found.

Bog roads are marvellous for walking. On fine summer days, the bogland hums, and the tarmac melts in the sun. The straight road, stretching into the distance, staggers in the heat.

On wet and misty days, the old bog road has another magic. Mist never dampened the Irish imagination. The veils of warm vapour that sweep in in summer off the western sea - "the mist becoming rain", as the poet Austin Clarke put it - are often enchanting, and the Irish rain inspiring, provided one doesn't have to be too long under it. The shower passes, and the world sparkles - "Brightness drenching through the branches", Clarke wrote.

West Cork, it is said, has 'no climate but much weather...' Sun and rain may come and go twenty times in a day. In this, there is much to be thankful for - never a boring moment, with the view changing constantly through the thick or thin lenses of water vapour. Light or gloom bathes the landscape as the sun sweeps a spotlight across it via gaps between the moving clouds. Indeed, the view disappears entirely, sometimes, and strangers won't believe it is there. Added to this are the diverse hues of the Irish countryside, the famous "forty shades of green".

So many flowers seasonally speckle or splash the roadside ditches that to mention the blooms of one month is enough. In July, purple loosestrife and orange montbretia brightens the verges. Montbretia is a perfect plant for these mountains, reminiscent of wild red hair. As a garden escapee, it is not listed as a wild flower in most books but, in fact, has colonised much of Ireland, especially river banks, lake sides and ditches. It is an attractive addition in both leaves and flowers, and the latter can be pressed in newspapers laid under a carpet to make a striking Christmas bouquet.

Tall, creamy meadowsweet is, in some years, so plentiful that, in car headlights, the verges look covered in froth. The head is made up of hundreds of tiny flowers. Elizabeth I apparently favoured it above other plants for the masking of Tudor smells, and she may well have had her pillows stuffed with the dried flowers both for their bouquet and for their soporific effect.

Part of an ancient Stone Row, Rathcool

Meadowsweet is not only sleep inducing, but a good painkiller, taken as an infusion. The name does not come from the fact that it grows in meadows and is sweet, but from the old name "mede-sweete' - it was used to flavour mead.

Some decades ago, when we lived in the West Cork hills and couldn't afford the pub, we made meadowsweet wine, which was light and a lovely yellow colour. What with the flower heads in your pillow and the fumes inside your head, it was easy to doze off of a winter's evening.

Workhouse railing, Schull

The peatland type around us is known as Atlantic blanket bog, and occurs where some rain falls on at least 235 days a year. In this area, between 1200mm and 1600 mm of rain is average. The formation of most bogs has been influenced in one way or another by humans since prehistory. I remember being impressed by the Greenland Inuits' knowledge of their environment upon learning that they have more than a hundred words to describe snow. However, I recently learned that in Irish there are 130 words relating to bogland and bogland species - no environmental duffers, we!

The low bushes on the bog fringes are sallows or pussy willows. Black bog rush is common, a plant which botanists agonise over because, elsewhere in Europe, it appears only in fens. Its growth in Irish bogs is thought to be made possible by westerly winds which bring it minerals in sea spray. Clumps of royal fern grow to a height of four or five feet in the waterlogged ground. Sheepsbit scabious is the blue flower of late summer, and bog cotton looks like tufts of cotton wool on stalks.

The water glitters in the sunlight, and pond skaters flit across the surface of the small pools. How these creatures find and colonise puddles in tractor tracks in the middle of fields is truly wonderful - find a pool, and you will almost certainly find a skater. They are predators, using long, pointed beaks to devour small flies that get trapped in the surface film.

On the pools' dark surface float white water lilies, perfect settings for drowned Ophelia, in the Pre-Raphelite painting. The large green lily pads would, of course, be ideal for squatting frogs but what frogs there are are unlikely to pose for us. We may see spawn, as early as January, as late as August. The frog populations of these uplands remain fairly stable, while amphibians of all kinds are seen less often elsewhere, not only in Ireland but globally. Radiation, due to the ozone holes, is a possible cause, along with pollutants in water. Here, in this poor mountain land, there is no silage run-off, or slurry spreading, so the water is relatively pure and unpolluted, although rich in oxides and minerals.

The lily flowers, floating between the round, shiny leaves, look eastern and exotic but are a native species. It is hard to believe such lovely plants were once employed as passion killers. In medieval times, a soup made from the seeds was used to quell the passions of too-ardent lovers; a long-suffering wife would slip a few in the stew, the better to stop the gallop of the husband. Drowned passion, one might say.

Bird life up here includes moorhens, or "water-hens" as they are called in Ireland. They paddle quietly amongst the rushes, surreptitious birds, clucking softly, black but for a bright red forehead 'shield', yellow tipped bill and white under-tail. Ravens fly overhead, easily told from rooks by their heavy, all-black beaks and shinier plumage. Grey crows, aka Hooded Crows or Scald Crows, are common, but will be exotic to the British visitor as they are not seen in England, Wales or southern Scotland, where there are Carrion Crows - not seen in Ireland - instead. They are handsome, robust birds, and will nest in low, stunted trees where there are no high trees available.

A few of the 130 words in Irish relating to bogs

The ruins of Schull workhouse and famine hospital 1850

(2) Barnancleeve, ('the basket shaped gap'), is half a mile dead ahead when we take a sharp left turn, signposted "Scoil Mhuire 3km", almost doubling back as we go south. Scoil Mhuire, the School of Mary, now Schull, is thought to be named for a monastic school established near St Mary's Church (see Colla Pier Walk) in pre-medieval times.

Now there are low rock escarpments on the right side, blotched with white lichens. God knows how old they are (as old as the stones themselves? - some tundra lichens live 10,000 years). Mountain sheep graze the green patches between the furze and heather, and amble across the road ahead. A plant in the roadside bog pools is called "redshank" (red legs) for the same reason as the estuary wader birds of the same name.

A right turning leads to a small reservoir. There is a private sign, but fishermen use the path. A roadside notice indicates where a season or day fishing licence may be obtained - £4 per day at the time of writing, no sweet corn or ground baiting allowed, maximum bag six trout. Fisher-persons may mark a "Creel census" card recording their catch.

A stream issues from the reservoir, which is a small lake dammed. Royal fern grows along it and sand martins (brown, with a white breast and brown collar) and house martins (black, with a white breast, no collar but a white rump) flit and swoop after flies. Tormentil, a pretty, yellow flower half the size of a buttercup, blooms riotously here from May until October. In Britain, it is also called Blood Root, the roots being used long ago to dye cloth red. Honeysuckle drapes the hedges, the berries bright red and gathered in tight clumps.

A road titled "Cul de Sac" leads off to the right. We pass it and now come out on big views over Coosheen Point, the headland at the eastern mouth of Schull Harbour, the Calf Islands and Cape Clear and Sherkin.

On this road, on Sundays, we regular encounter skeins of men out for a walk, not for their health or for the scenery but to follow the road bowlers ("boughlers", as they are called in the West Cork tongue). "Boughling" is taken very seriously; hundreds, even thousands of pounds are wagered on a match or 'score', or even on a throw. If the bowlers have already passed, divots or sops on the road will map their progress; these are either placed to mark where a throw reaches, or to provide a "mark" for the bowler to aim for in order to camber his shot around a corner. Sometimes, the 28 oz iron ball is "lofted" over a corner. Great skill is involved. Two places in Ireland - Armagh and West Cork - are 'cradles' of the sport; the only other road bowling tradition in Europe is in South Germany. Perhaps the Celts, passing through Germany before reaching Ireland, left the tradition behind. Women attend the serious matches, and there are some fine women bowlers. But up here on ordinary Sunday afternoons, it's mainly men and boys.

A few fields in to the left, below the road, is the site of two boulder burials, boulders laid flat on three supporting stones. Radio carbon readings date them at about 3080 BP (Before the Present). They can be seen from the road, but not easily in spring or summer, for the herbage that abounds.

We see a group of Scots pines on the left - three in a row, and an isolated tree. In the springtime bog, there are stands of flag irises, a lovely yellow flower, originally the emblem of the Franks in Roman times, later the 'fleur de lys', or flower of Louis, because it was displayed on his banners at the Crusades.

Otter

After crossing the small stone bridge, we turn sharp left, but, 50 yards before, on the right hand ditch, we may find a break of 'hurts', as they are called, whortleberries, or bilberries, quite delicious when ripe. The green veined stems bear single fruits, like small black currants. In the field behind, one may see stonechats, colourful sparrow-size birds, given to perching on fence posts and bush tops, the male very striking with his black head, white collar and russet breast, the femalc similar but much paler. They seem always to be in pairs, and are very local and territorial.

(3) Crossing the stone bridge, we swing sharp left, following a babbling stream, alongside which montbretia and ramsons - 'wild garlic' - grow. Hereabouts, bird song fills the air in springtime, chiffchaffs warble, robins thrill. The road is very pleasant, going downhill. The stream turns off and, soon, we see a tin barn ahead, with an old cottage behind it. The road goes left, with fuschia hedges again, and interesting wrought iron gates, one bearing the words "Anam Cara" ("soul friend", a spiritual 'way' based on an old Gaelic concept) Another brightly painted with, I believe, a bee motif. The stream again accompanies us, bridged to houses, one called "Rippling Rill", an old name for a brook popular, I think, with the Lake Poets. Christine Thery, the illustrator of this book, remembers often seeing otters on the road when she lived here. So, keep an eye out.

Passing the 30 mph sign, we reach the main Schull-Ballydehob road, where a wide grass verge leads us safely back to our starting point at the Workhouse corner, a hundred yards along.

Schull Point and Colla

Schull Pier - the Foreshore Walk - St Mary's Church ruins and Famine Graveyard - Colla Pier and high land above.

Locality: OS Sheet 88 starting in square 9231, at the children's playground in Schull.

Description and Distance: A loop walk, 7 km., 3½ mls.

Walking Time: including viewing church and graveyard, 2½ hrs.

Walking conditions: Paths, bohreens and back roads. Some steep - but short - stretches.

Features: This is a walk full of variety, and sea and mountain air. We begin at sea level, with piers and boats, the seashore and rock pools. We ascend gently to elevated views of Roaringwater Bay, Long Island, the Calf Islands, Sherkin and Cape Clear. In good weather, Fastnet Rock, due south, and Mizen Head, to the west, can be seen. There is a sense of space and wildness on the hills above Colla.

Flora and fauna: The shoreline rocks and pools teem with life in summer and will fascinate children and amateur marine biologists for hours. Gulls, kittiwakes, cormorants, gannets, oystercatchers and ringed plover are amongst the sea birds; inland, kestrels, ravens, grey crows, stonechats and larks may be seen. Seals occasionally come close to shore. Rabbits are seen in the evening, hares in early mornings in spring. Foxes and stoats are not unusual.

Equipment: Everyday shoes, but one may need to pick one's step after rain.

Itinerary:

(1) We set out from the children's playground below the municipal car park at the east end of the town, opposite the road signposted for Bantry, Glengarriff and Durrus.

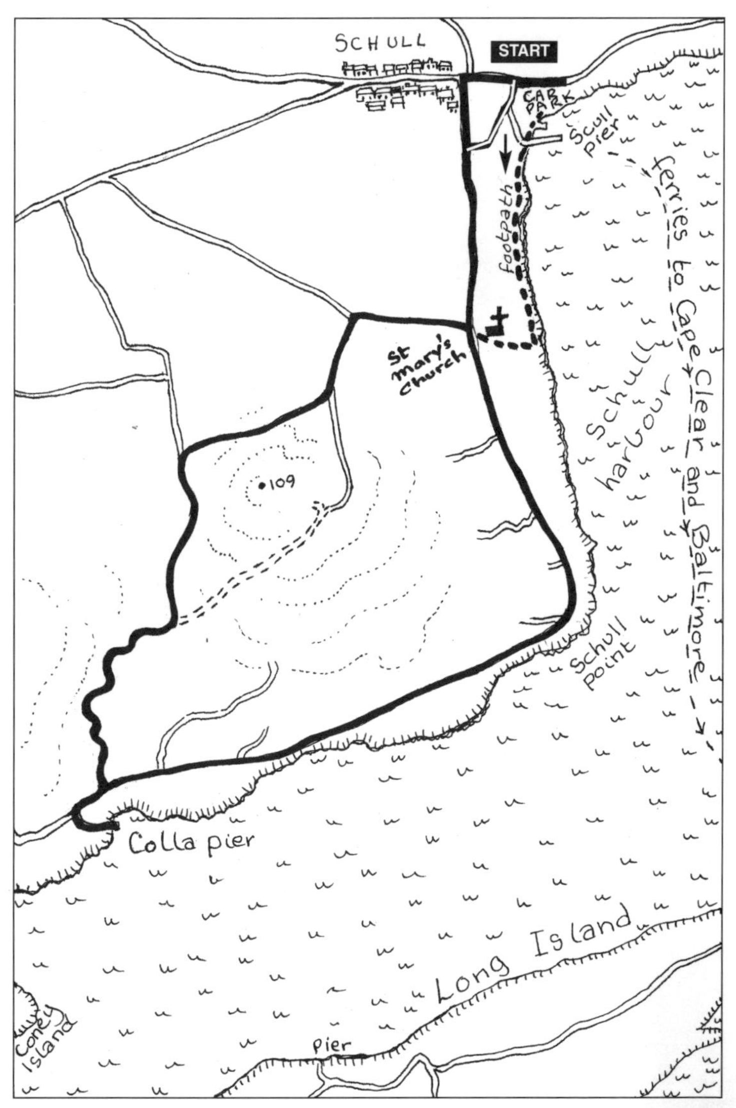

The uplands above Colla, Colla Pier, Schull Point and town

Leaving the playground via the concrete path at the bottom corner right, we descend towards the pier. The path crosses a short bridge, with a stream gurgling below. The banks are overgrown with red stemmed Japanese knotweed, aka "japweed", an exotic member of the dock family. Not a very pretty plant, its importation into Irish gardens was not a good idea - it shortly bolted from the borders and sprouted on the lawns. Generations of gardeners have attacked it with hoes, flame-throwers and noxious substances to little avail. Today, it thrives robustly on waste ground and roadsides.

Long island houses (like children's drawings of houses)

Here, by the stream, some fine fuschia also blooms. Fuschia is another introduction - from New Zealand and South America - but its liberty is welcomed, not reviled. A fuschia flower was recently adopted as the symbol of West Cork Tourism, somewhat ironically in that road-widening measures have cut down many of the famous fuschia 'corridors'. Children suck nectar from the neck of the flower. It doesn't seem to do them any harm.

There is a large concrete reproduction of an ammonite on the path just before the pier. This well-intentioned 'art in the landscape' apparently fell apart shortly after it was installed. I've been told that the sigh of relief from some 'discerning' Schull residents could be heard in Ballydehob.

The pier is often bright as a postcard with multicoloured nets and ropes. As many as fifty yachts and ten fishing boats may be moored nearby. The commercial boats catch lobster and crab inshore or trawl for white fish in the Celtic Sea. The failure of successive Irish governments to invest in fishing is evidenced in the sorry state of the boats. Meat barons, tribunal lawyers and big farmers may be able to afford yachts; fishermen, largely, own tubs.

From the pier, ferries cross to Baltimore, Sherkin and Cape Clear Island , and offer passengers a voyage through Carbery's Hundred Isles. Schull's yawl rowers - All Ireland Champions, 1997 - may sometimes be seen skimming the harbour, only touching the surface in spots.

Stoat on a wall

(2) A finger post at the top of the pier directs us to the "Foreshore Walk", a concrete path winding along the harbour edge, with small coves and wave platforms below us on the shore. Steps descend to these, at intervals. In summer, the rock pools are a delight, full of shannies, blennies, butterfish, pipe fish, scorpion fish, brittle stars, shrimps and crabs. Most obvious will be the shannies, comical little fish, somehow reminiscent of puppies, with big eyes set high in their hatchet-shaped heads and fins like small legs upon which they can scurry from pool to pool as the tide recedes. In the breeding season, sociable groups may be found under rocks, on the wet sand, where they remain out of water until the tide returns.

Opposite us, is the harbour's eastern shore, with Cosheen Point at the mouth. The islands beyond are a constant presence. We will get higher views later, when they can be better identified and discussed.

Soon, a stile and small bridge are crossed and we are in the field below the graveyard. Beside the hedge, a narrow concrete path climbs the field. We may take it now - or continue for another twenty yards to a small cove reached via a second stile and bridge over a stream which, in summer, is almost hidden by bindweed, with white trumpet-like flowers. On a fine day, it is pleasant to sit here and watch the sea. The shale on the 'beach' provides perfect 'skimmers', which enthusiasts, young and old, can enjoy.

Returning over the stile, we take the path up the field edge towards the ruined church. The slope is gentle, the concrete thoughtfully scored to give a good grip. From spring to autumn, the hedge is full of flowers, celandine, gorse and honeysuckle, blackthorn, whitethorn and elder blossom. In late summer, given the right mix of sun and rain, the blackberries here are full and luscious. There is nothing like a juicy blackberry warmed by the sun. In September, there are still foxgloves and orange montbretia, and creamy honeysuckle draped on the briars.

(3) We step over a stile into the upper field. The ruins are of a rebuilt St Mary's Church of Ireland, completed in 1720 - decretal letters evidence a pre-reformation (Catholic) church on the site four centuries earlier. An 'ogee' window in the left wall - tall and narrow, with a pointed arch - is probably a surviving artefact from this building.

A Famine Graveyard lies below the church. To reach it, we cross the modern cemetery to the tussocky ground beyond. Here, there are many worn and fallen headstones The Great Famine, 1845 -1848, devastated the Mizen Peninsula and, according to an account of 1874, "...the graveyard at Schull

Schull foreshore

was doubled in size to receive upwards to half the population in a single year." The population of 17,000 in 1841 fell to 6,000 by 1851.

A large stone, carved in the old Irish script with 'fadas' and 'seimhiús', commemorates the famine dead. A Tipperary curate, in a letter to the 'Examiner' in 1847, noted that "...if the Protestants are in a state which Captain Caffin describes (i.e. 'dying of absolute starvation') what must be the condition of the Roman Catholics? It is well known that in every part of Ireland, the Protestants are a wealthier class than the Roman Catholics."

The imposing tomb of the Rev. Dr. Robert Traill is above the graveyard, beneath the arched window, perhaps a case of 'nearer my God to Thee'. Vicar of Schull during the famine years, he was a grandfather of John Millington Synge, playwright of "Riders to the Sea" and "Playboy of the Western World". Dr Traill, the Examiner letter notes, admitted to being in ignorance of "the real state of the people" but apparently afterwards contributed to famine relief. Danno O'Mahony, a World Wrestling Champion, is also buried here. A fine Celtic cross, delicately carved and supporting a robust growth of yellow lichen, stands to the left of the window. Making our way around to the right, we find more examples of fine monumental sculpture.

St Mary's Church, Schull

There are curiosities amongst the crypts, mention of a girl who died in a Napoleonic tower, mention of a woman who seemed to have outlived her husband by 60 years. There is the tomb of the Hull family, British appointed landlords of the area for 300 years. In 1798, the Year of the French, members of the family, while out walking near Schull, spotted the French fleet of 35 ships en route to assist Wolfe Tone and the United Irishmen. They raised the alarm and a British militia was sent to repel them at Bantry Bay. In the event, what the militia could not have effected storms did, and the French were, literally, blown out of the bay. The scholarly, morbid or sentimental may find this bone yard fascinating for hours.

(4) Upon exiting onto the road, we walk left. I debated recommending going right, then left, and left again, opposite "Foxglove", to reach the hill above the town via the gentler slope of the tarred road - in other words doing the 'upland leg' in reverse, approaching the hills from inland and descending with the view of the islands ahead. However, after writing both options, I decided that to climb the hills from the sea was most attractive. But walkers will enjoy either route.

As we emerge from the churchyard and walk west, the cemetery wall is worth inspection for its fine examples of navelwort, hard fern and spleenwort, a small, lacy fern with leaves like beadlets strung along the stems. These ferns have no flowers; the spores are on the veins beneath the leaves.

On the left is a garden with gunnera , "giant rhubarb" as we called it as children when, avoiding its spiked stems, we sat under the huge leaves and imagined ourselves in the Amazon. It dies back in winter, and may be barely noticed as we pass. There are fine houses on both sides of the road, and high escalonia hedges here and there, mixed with fuschia; both survive salt gales very well. A small, stone house on the right boasts an enormous, and very beautiful, wrought iron gate.

On a right hand curve, we pass a swathe of green verge with a quarry behind it, down which some heather grows. There are mature houses here, often with big trees and lawns. Cordyline palms, natives of Australia, thrive all along this Gulf Stream coast, where there is little frost. "African grasses" are another items of exotica. At the gateway of a house on the left, there is a myrtle, with red bark, waxy leaves and white flowers.

Now, the trees are left behind and the coast is windswept and 'natural', with views out over the Celtic Sea and the islands that guard the entrance to Roaring Water Bay. Nearest to us is the north eastern tip of Long Island, with its gleaming white beacon, dramatic in the sunlight, more so when spray is thrown over it by breaking waves. Beyond it, are the three Calf Islands, and south of these, Clear Island, Oileán Cléire. These days, people often call it Cape Clear Island - perhaps it sounds more romantic, and sells better.

We cross a humpback bridge and now the road is very straight, with scrubby outcrops of gorse and heather on either side, and a fine view of Long Island, below.

Long Island is close inshore; at one time, farmers swam cattle across behind their boats to Schull fair. The island wives were powerful oarswomen, and would row as far as Skibbereen to the mill. On December 20th, 1795, a brig on her way from Cadiz to Dublin with a cargo of oranges - for Christmas? - foundered in the Channel and was attacked by the good citizens with axes so that "not an atom was left afloat". In 1838, a bullion ship perished nearby, spilling valuable cargo, including seven silver plates weighing a hundredweight each, onto the sea bed, keeping divers at work for eight years.

It is said that, in the 1940's, a local man invented a wind-propelled delivery service in the form of a small self-steering sailboat that could be launched and sent to and from the island carrying light goods.

In 1973, special postage stamps were designed for the Long Island Carriage Service, another local transport initiative. 60,000 sets were printed before the National Post Office had publication banned.

After the straight stretch, a narrow road turns up to the right, between a newly built house and a small plantation of fir trees. A finger post indicates 'Toad Hall Kennels'. We should, for the moment, 'overshoot' this road, to go a hundred yards further to Colla Pier. We will return to it.

At the gable of a traditional house, we turn down the steep, curving road to Colla Pier. It is a pleasant, quiet place, worth the visit. A few, small colourful boats are tied up, and some yachts are moored offshore. Holidaymakers swim and children fish here in summer but the water is deep at full tides.

Colla serves Midland pier across the channel on Long Island, and the townlands have long been connected. The island population, however, has greatly declined. In 1871, 40 houses were occupied; now, only 6 of those families still keep a foothold. But cottages are being renovated for holiday homes, of which there are already many in Schull.

One summer day, as we sat on the pier, a van arrived and disgorged two German lady holidaymakers with suitcases. Shortly afterwards, a boat arrived from the island, complete with - as the song goes - a handsome boatman to ferry them over, a young Englishman, with his dog.

(5) We retrace our steps to the plantation, and turn left beside it. Gunnera grows in the garden on the right. A pretty, traditional house is straight ahead. The road curves around behind it and the land soon becomes hillocky. Grass grows up the middle of the road. We climb a short, steep hill, past a farmhouse where dogs bark while wagging their tails, towards two new houses above. The road here is very bad, furrowed and broken by winter rains, but it is great walking country. We have doubled back over the lower road and are in the 'highlands'. The silence of the hills surrounds us. Although well walked, this track is private and ramblers owe access to the hospitality of local people.

We gently climb higher, through hairpin bends, and look out over acres of gorse and heather to the sea and the islands. The scenery is as wild and lovely as anywhere in Ireland, with a breathtaking view on a clear day and a magical view at sunset when the house on small Coney Island is cut out in silhouette against the silvered sea. Further west, the thin arm of Croagh Bay lies between dark rounded hills On this winding road, one finds oneself facing west, then north, then east, then south. The islands of Roaring Water Bay, big Olieán Cléire and Sherkin, the heights of Mallavoge, Mizen Peak, Mount Gabriel or Coomfarna, all, at some point, fill the horizon. On bad days, when the view closes in, it is a romantic spot from which to watch the white surf leap and piggyback onto the black islands.

On the OS map, it will be seen that the track divides, one branch going due north following longitude 92. We take this branch which is, in fact, the 'pista' or gravelled surface. The branch going straight ahead, south of the Spot Height 109, is largely grassed over.

Along the way, we notice that some quarrying has been carried on. Sometimes, these scoops in the rock are colonised by hosts of flowers -

white oxeye daisies, golden buttercups, blue sheepsbit, purple foxgloves or "fairy thimbles". The moor and heathland is fragmented, broken up, not a square yard the same, a land of many shapes and colours. Meadow pipits are common, and larks, although now rare everywhere, are seen. Overhead, one sometimes sees a hunting kestrel hanging in the sky. Once, a weasel crossing the track paused to look at me, standing on hind feet. 'Weasels' or 'waesals' (they are properly called Irish stoats) are famously curious. Very beautiful, with a bright red coat and pure white belly, black tipped tail and beady eyes, they are not at all likely to run up one's trousers as some folk say. After a good look at me, mine scampered off across the road and flowed up a stone wall, like a brown snake.

Spectacular Kerry spotted slugs are encountered, lusitanian creatures endemic in Iberia but uniquely found in Ireland's south west. They can stretch to 12cm, almost 5 inches and, unlike other slugs - which contract - they curl into a ball if disturbed. Shaded charcoal-colour with white spots when living in the open, or bronze or golden when forest dwellers, they graze on lichens, mosses and algae, and lay two dozen eggs in June.

At a gate, we reach "The Bell Tower", a fine house, with a gazebo perched on a salient in the field below it, looking west. The overseas owner previously had two notices announcing 'private', one of them warning that Public Liability Insurance was not in place. It is still not widely known - or, in some cases, known but not admitted - that since the 1995 Occupier's Liability Act it is virtually impossible for a trespasser or even an invited user to sue a landowner for damages. Only contractors working on the land can hope to bring a successful action and owners should have public liability in respect of these. When we last passed, the 'private' notices were gone - I imagine few walkers have ever trespassed. The gate across the road may be closed but somebody has thoughtfully installed a stile.

Shortly beyond the gate, we pass a lovely house where the owner has planted a pair of imaginative "standing stones" in his garden. They look extremely authentic but are, in fact, the work of a local JCB artist, Mr John McCarthy. Indeed, elsewhere in the garden, and by the same artist, there is an enchanting "stone circle" in the shade of some sycamores, but this is not visible from the lane. We cross a cattle grid, and the track changes ownership. The owner of the new section is also hospitable, and has no objection to walkers. At the time of writing, his fine, white puck goat is a striking feature on the hillside.

(6) Now, about 5km from our starting point, we again reach Council-maintained tarred road. We turn sharp right, downhill, towards Schull. The road is narrow and pretty, wide enough for just one car, with grass growing up the middle. We come out on panoramic views over Schull Harbour, with the boats and islands. Downhill we go, now rewarded for the climbs on the outward journey. We arrive at a guest house, Stanley Lodge, and another, Stanley House, and bear right around its gable. After passing under some trees, we arrive at a T junction; with a house called Foxglove opposite. Here, we turn right and shortly see St. Mary's Church again, straight ahead.

We turn left at the ruins, and approach the town, passing St Mary's Hospital, with its view of the sea, and Schull Planetarium and the Fastnet Marine Education Centre on the grounds of Schull Community College.

Grove House is a lovely residence on the left, with twin driveways sweeping up to the front door. It was once a hotel patronised by the literati, including George Bernard Shaw and JM Synge, precursors perhaps of the present Schull holidaymakers - Maeve Binchy, et al - from media-land Dublin 4. It is a fine house, with five windows on the upper, four on the lower, floor, peeping through mantles of Virginia creeper. It was built by one Rev. Triphook, circa 1880, for his daughter. He is buried in St. Mary's, inside the church.

We shortly pass the nearby C of I Church of the Holy Trinity, where Triphook was rector, then a complex of holiday cottages, each named for a bird. A hundred yards later, we emerge at a T-junction at the western end of Schull main street. Here, at the corner of the Old Bank House, and opposite a pub called The Tigín, we turn right and walk down Schull's colourful artery. There are many opportunities for post-amble coffees or warming draughts before we arrive at the car park where we began.